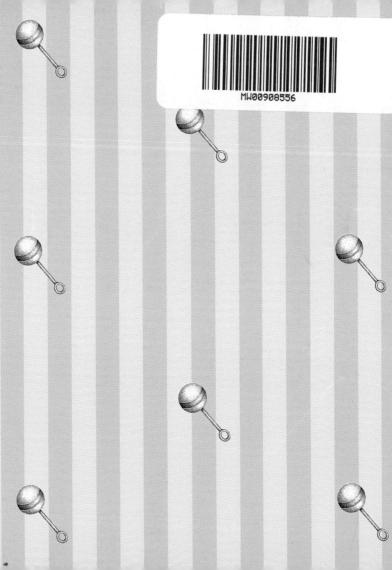

Fairy Kisses and Stork Bites

Amazing, Adorable Facts About Babies

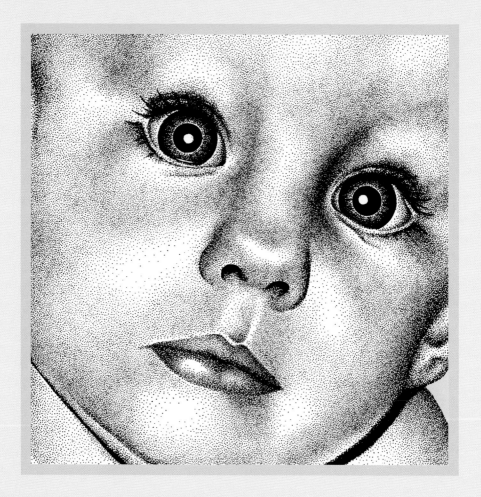

Fairy Kisses
and
Stork Bites

Amazing, Adorable Facts
About Babies

Written and Illustrated by
Karen Brown

**Andrews McMeel
Publishing**

Kansas City

00 01 02 03 TWP 10 9 8 7 6 5 4 3 2 1

ISBN: 0-7407-0468-0

Library of Congress Card Number: 99-068448

www.karenbrowndesign.com/fairykisses

ATTENTION: SCHOOLS AND BUSINESSES

For my mother,
Mary.

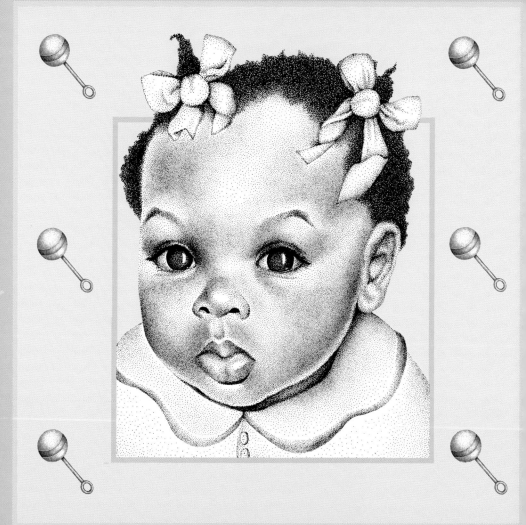

Acknowledgments

No baby comes into this world on its own and neither does any book.

First thanks go to my friends: Melissa Horton, Joycelyn Calvin White, Wendy Mitchell, Joyce Victor, Greg Holzman, Mark Fox and Denise Lawson (who as I write this are expecting their first), and Ani and Richard Couch, all of whom kept me going with their kind attention and baby pictures. A very special thanks to my cover model, the lovely Sophie Helf, and her parents, Rick and Ramona.

All love to my sister, Janet, and Marty and Bo for their understanding and support.

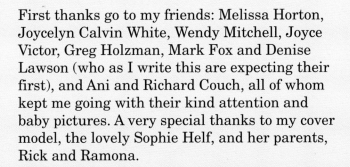

I want to thank my smart and slinky agent, Betsy Amster, for her help and encouragement all along the way. Likewise to my fine editor at Andrews McMeel, Chris Schillig, who gave me so much respect and creative freedom.

There's no adequate way to express my bewildered thanks to Mike Leonard of the *Today* show for his inexplicable continued interest in my progress and for giving me, like a present wrapped up in a big red bow, my first national exposure.

And lastly, for helping me learn to draw what little bit I am able to, all gratitude to our greatest living illustrator, Mr. Jim Woodring.

FAIRY KISSES & STORK BITES &

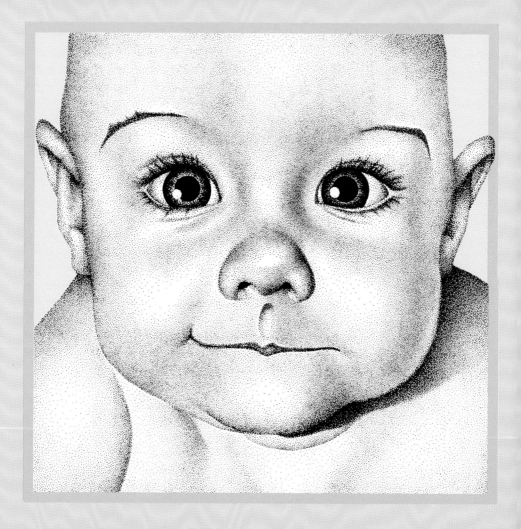

What was the
biggest year of the
baby boom?

1957,
when 4,300,000 babies
were born in the
United States.

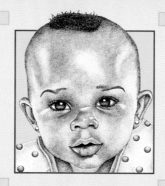

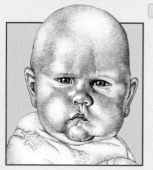

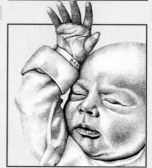

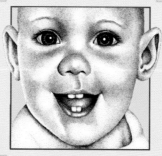
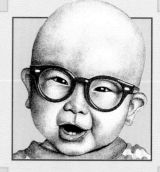

Who gave birth to the most babies?

In the 18th century, Mrs. Feodor Vassilyev,
a Russian peasant woman, gave birth to 69 children
conceived in 27 separate pregnancies. She had 16 pairs
of twins, 7 sets of triplets, and 4 sets of quadruplets.
All but two of these children survived infancy.

*What is the record for the most sets of triplets born to
one mother?*

In the middle of the last century, an Italian woman
named Maddalena Granata gave birth to 15 sets
of triplets—yes, that's 45 babies.

What is the most common baby name worldwide?

Mohammed.

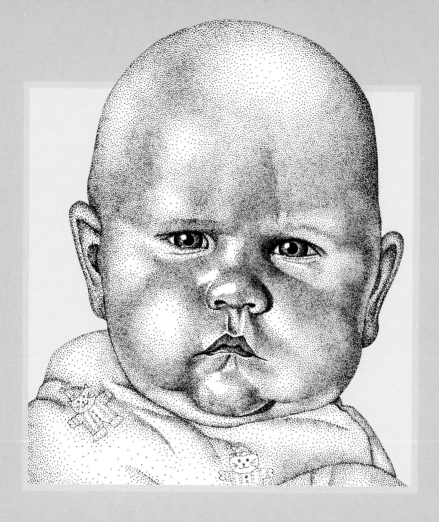

How heavy was
the biggest baby
ever born?

23 pounds,
12 ounces.
His mother was
7 feet, 5 1/2
inches tall.

How many diapers will a baby use before it is toilet trained?

About 5,000.

If those diapers were placed end-to-end, how far would they reach?

A disposable diaper is about 15 inches long, so they would extend 6,250 feet—approximately the length of 20 football fields.

If you stacked them, how high would they reach?

A disposable diaper is about 3/4 inches thick, so they would make a stack approximately 312 feet high—about the height of a 20-story office building.

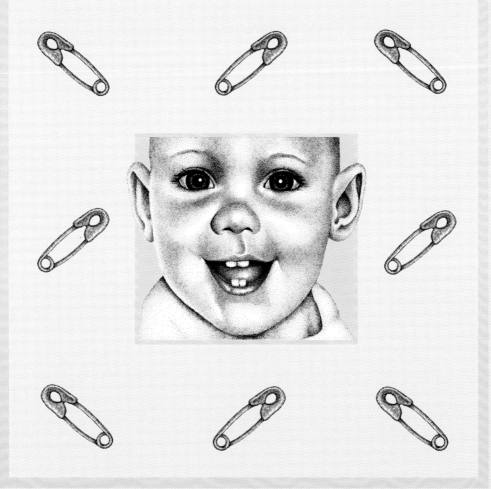

If you piled up all the (clean) diapers a baby uses before it is toilet trained, how much would they weigh?

A disposable diaper weighs about three ounces, so a baby's lifetime allotment of 5,000 diapers would weigh 937 pounds, nearly half a ton.

What percentage of American parents use disposable diapers?

Around 90 percent.

*During the first two months of life,
how often will the
average baby need changing?*

About once an hour.

How tall is a newborn baby compared to its expected adult height?

An adult
will grow
up to be
slightly
over
three
times its
height
as a
newborn.

Who weighs more at birth— boys or girls?

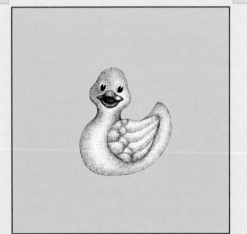

Boys are generally a little heavier and a little longer.

Who stays in the womb longer—boys or girls?

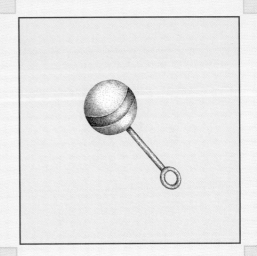

Girls—
by about
five days.

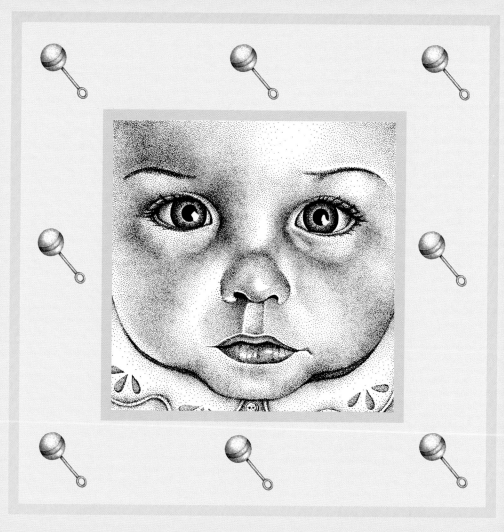

Who invented the baby carriage?

Charles Burton introduced the first commercially manufactured baby carriage in 1848 in New York City. When pedestrians complained of being run into by the carriages, Burton fled to England where he opened a "perambulator" factory. His business became a success, helped in part by the patronage of Queen Victoria, one of his first clients.

At what age might a baby start to suck its thumb?

Some babies suck their thumbs extremely early in life, even in the womb. It may be the earliest regular habit a baby can develop.

When will a baby learn to pick up objects with its thumb and forefinger?

Known as the pincer grasp, this skill develops around nine to 10 months.

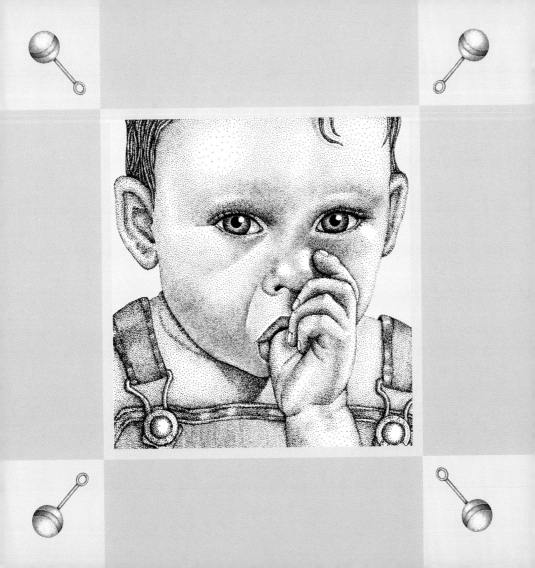

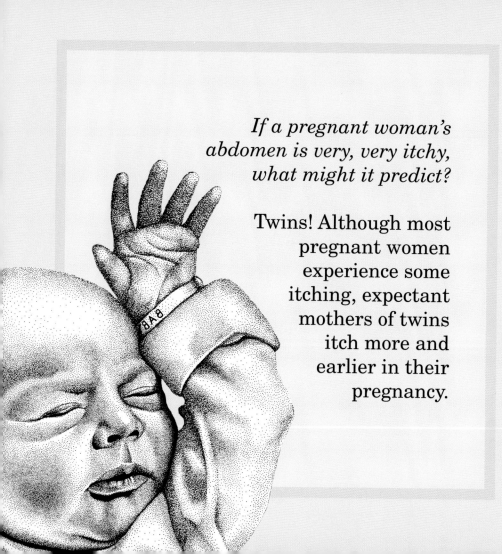

If a pregnant woman's abdomen is very, very itchy, what might it predict?

Twins! Although most pregnant women experience some itching, expectant mothers of twins itch more and earlier in their pregnancy.

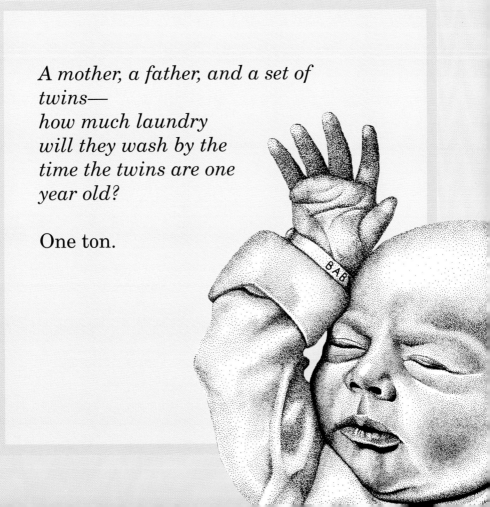

A mother, a father, and a set of twins—
how much laundry
will they wash by the
time the twins are one
year old?

One ton.

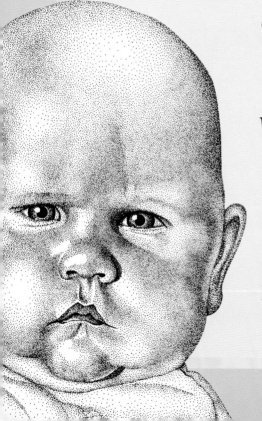

How heavy were the biggest twins ever born?

They had a combined weight of 27 pounds, 12 ounces.

What makes identical twins identical?

Identical twins are the result of a single egg that splits in two after being fertilized. Identical twins share the same genes.

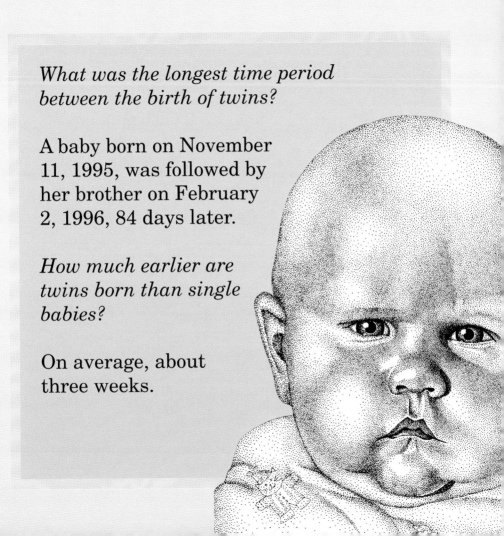

What was the longest time period between the birth of twins?

A baby born on November 11, 1995, was followed by her brother on February 2, 1996, 84 days later.

How much earlier are twins born than single babies?

On average, about three weeks.

Who wrote the classic children's lullaby "Rock-a-Bye Baby"?

Charles Dupree Blake, 1846–1903.

At what age will a baby smile in response to your smile?

There's a lot of debate about what constitutes a real smile and what is "just gas," but usually a baby will smile back at you somewhere around two months of age.

What is a cherub?

A cherub is a member of the second order of angels, often represented as a beautiful, rosy-checked baby with wings.

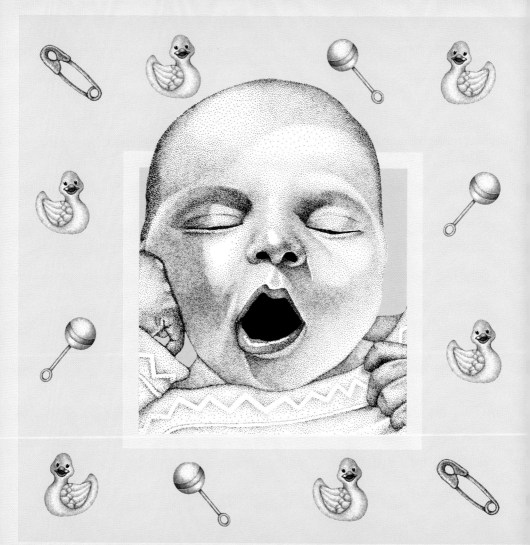

Do babies dream?

Yes. About half of a newborn baby's sleep is REM or Rapid Eye Movement sleep that indicates dreaming. So babies do indeed dream, but we will never, ever know what they dream about.

How much does a baby sleep during the first month of life?

About 16 to 23 hours a day.

What are "fairy kisses"?

When a baby smiles or frowns in its sleep, it is being kissed by fairies, according to Welsh folklore.

What are "stork bites"?

Stork bites are pink areas around a newborn baby's forehead, eyelids, or the back of the neck. These marks usually fade within a few months after birth. These marks are called stork bites because it looks as though the stork took a few loving nibbles before lowering the baby down the chimney.

What was the first nationally marketed baby cereal?

Pablum, introduced in 1928.

When will a baby grow a full head of hair?

Some babies are born with one, although most newborn hair will fall out and grow in again, sometimes in a different color or texture. Fair, light-haired babies tend to stay bald longer, but nearly all children have hair to be proud of by the time they are two years old.

At what age does a baby see as well as an adult?

Babies develop most of their adult vision by the time they are one year old.

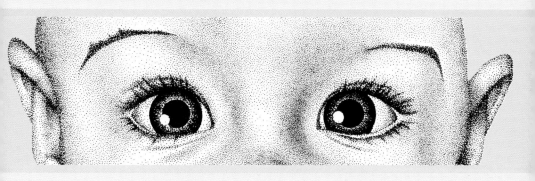

How far away can a newborn infant focus its eyes?

About 12 to 18 inches, or approximately the distance between a breastfeeding infant and its mother's face.

When does a baby's eye color stop changing?

A baby's eye color will stabilize in about three months but may still change during the entire first year of life.

Why are pink and blue "baby colors"?

The origins of these colors are so ancient that we may never know for certain what spiritual or protective function they once served. And while pink and blue are traditional colors for boys and girls in Western culture, they are by no means universal. For example, baby boys in China may be dressed in red for good fortune. According to some very sweet European folklore, pink and blue are babies' natural choices because boys are born in blue cabbages and girls are born in pink roses.

What percentage of babies are born flat-footed?

One hundred percent. Underdeveloped muscles and a pad of fat under the arch make virtually all babies' feet look flat. As the child grows and begins walking, normal arches usually always develop.

At what age does a baby begin to walk?

The general rule is "first steps on the first birthday," but many perfectly normal babies begin walking before or after age one.

What is the best surface for a baby to take its first steps on?

Babies generally learn most easily when they are able to walk barefoot indoors. This way they can learn safely, get some traction, and feel the floor beneath their feet.

When should a baby get its first pair of shoes?

Socks and knitted booties can help keep little feet warm, but a baby doesn't need real shoes until walking is well established and the baby is walking outdoors.

Who was the first baby born in the White House?

James Madison Randolph, on January 17, 1806. He was the grandson of Thomas Jefferson and the son of Jefferson's daughter, Martha Jefferson Randolph.

Who was the first baby born in the White House to a United States president?

Esther Cleveland, on September 9, 1893. She was the daughter of President Grover Cleveland and Francis Folsom Cleveland. Grover Cleveland was the first and only president married in the White House.

Who was the only baby born to a president-elect?

John Fitzgerald Kennedy Jr., who was born on November 25, 1960.

What is nipple confusion?

Nipple confusion occurs when a breast-fed baby won't nurse after it has been using a pacifier or a bottle. The baby becomes confused because the sucking action on a breast is different from sucking on a synthetic nipple.

What organization maintains an international nonprofit network that provides advice and encouragement to women who want to breast-feed?

The La Leche League.

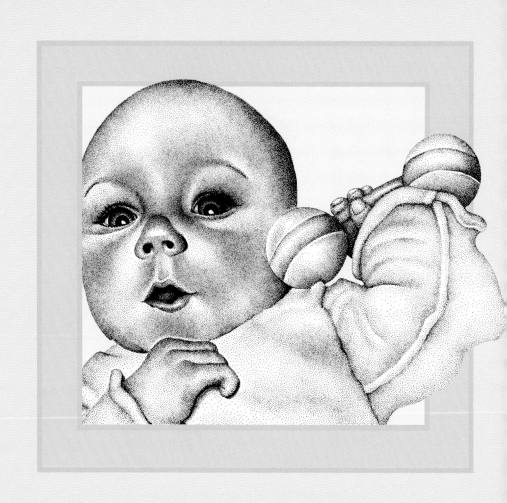

What is the grasp reflex?

The grasp reflex is believed to be an instinctive impulse that helps an infant hold on tightly to its parent. Many new parents are astonished by their newborn baby's remarkable strength the first time it squeezes an adult finger.

What percentage of babies are born left-handed?

The same as the general population—about 10 percent. More boys are left-handed than girls. Very young babies may seem ambidextrous, but a bias for using a particular hand usually begins to develop as the baby grows.

When does a baby typically say its first word?

Although some parents are certain their very special baby could speak within days or weeks of being born, most babies speak their real first words around 12 months of age.

What were the baby Buddha's first words immediately after being born?

"Worlds above, worlds below, there's no one in the world like me." Perhaps this is the message in every baby's first cry.

At what age does a baby laugh out loud for the first time?

Usually around four months.

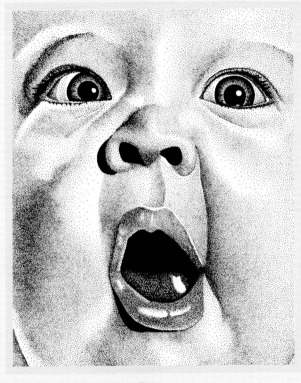

When is a baby most likely to show symptoms of colic?

Starting around the second or third week of life, about 20 percent of babies will be "colicky," which means that they cry *a lot* and sometimes simply cannot be comforted. The causes of colic are not well understood but the symptoms generally pass after three months of age.

Why do babies cry during airplane flights?

On takeoff and landing, many otherwise content babies begin to yell. This is because changes in aircraft pressure painfully unbalance the air-filled cavity of the baby's sensitive middle ear.

What is "magic breath"?

Some people believe that breathing gently on the top of a baby's head will calm it down and quiet its tears. This is called "magic breath."

Who has the longer umbilical cord— boys or girls?

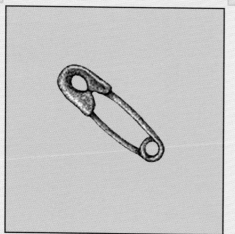

Boys— by about two inches.

Who learns to walk and talk sooner— boys or girls?

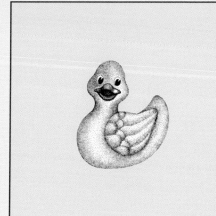

Girls— generally a few weeks sooner than boys.

How old was the oldest new mother?

A woman who was 63 years, 9 months old gave birth to a daughter on November 7, 1996.

Statistically, the fewest birth complications arise when the mother is what age?

Twenty-two.

What percentage of babies in the United States are delivered by cesarean?

Almost 25 percent. In 1970, it was 5.5 percent.

Which country was the first to register births on a regular basis?

Canada was the first country to record births systematically, which it has been doing since 1621. It is the only country in the world with a comprehensive collection of birth records spanning more than three centuries.

At what age does a baby "discover" its own hands?

Starting around two to three months of age, a baby discovers it has hands and may spend hours each day sucking on them or staring at them.

At what age does a baby learn to transfer a toy from one hand to another?

Usually around four to five months.

When and where was the first baby show?

The first baby show, featuring 127 infant contestants, was held in Springfield, Ohio, in 1859.

*Where
was the
world's
first day
care center
and when
did it
open?*

The first
children's day
nursery for
working mothers was opened in
Paris in 1844.

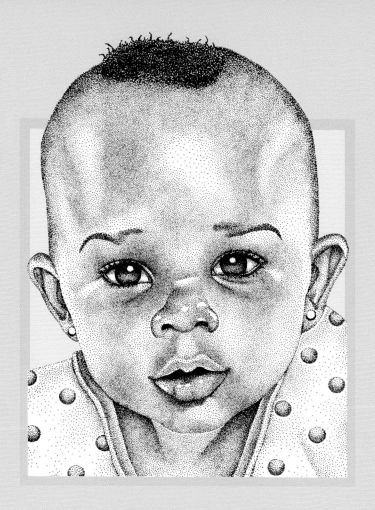

Can the sound of a baby's cry stimulate the flow of its mother's milk?

It certainly can. Some mothers are so responsive that their milk will begin to flow if they hear *any* baby crying, even on television. In fact, some mothers have had their milk stimulated by the mewing of a cat!

Can a woman who has never been pregnant breast-feed an adopted baby?

Incredibly, yes. Many adoptive mothers have lactated naturally and successfully nursed babies. Some mothers need to provide supplements for complete nutrition, but many develop a full milk supply for their babies.

How long is the average labor for a first birth?

First babies, on average, are born after about 14 hours of labor.

How long does it take for a new mother to recover from childbirth?

Every birth and every mother are different. Depending on the ease or difficulty of the delivery, major recovery is usually well under way two to four weeks after birth. It is important to remember, however, that the baby needed nine months to prepare for birth and the new mother may need a good nine months after giving birth before she feels fully recovered, emotionally and physically.

How much
does
a baby's
brain
grow in
weight
in the
first year?

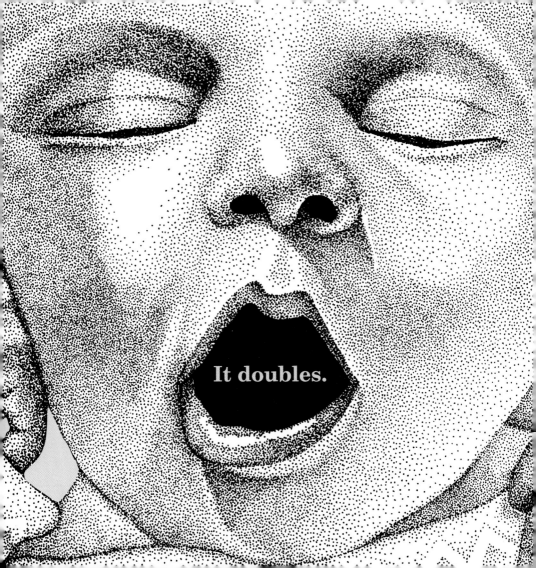

What percentage of a newborn baby is fat?

About 16 percent.

By the time a baby is one year old, how much will it have grown in weight since it was born?

A baby's weight roughly triples between birth and its first birthday.

Will a chubby baby grow up to be fat?

Probably not. Only about one in five "fat" babies grow up to become overweight adults.

Is it ever normal for a baby to lose weight?

Yes. Nearly all babies lose weight, usually about 5 percent to 10 percent of their birth weight, in the first five days after being born. After that, the baby should begin to gain weight again.

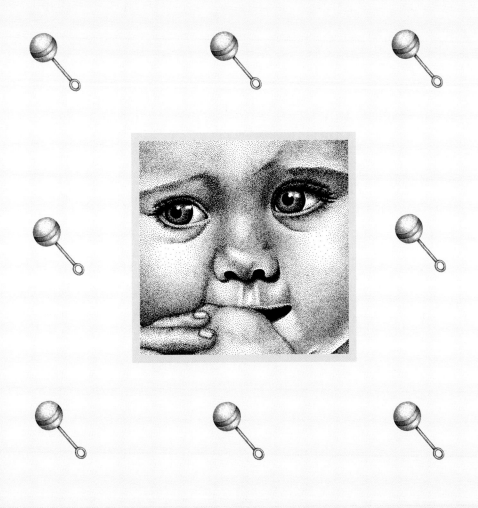

What real-life baby was born in a house with 365 rooms, one for each day of the year, and 52 staircases, one for each week of the year?

Vita Sackville-West, the owner and designer of the gardens at Sissinghurst Castle. She was born on March 9, 1892, at Knole, the largest house in England.

What mythological baby twins were raised by wolves?

Romulus and Remus.

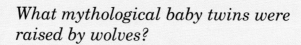

Who was the baby Achilles and what did his mother do to him?

Achilles grew up to become the greatest warrior of the Trojan War. Reacting to a grim prophecy, his mother held the baby Achilles by his heel and dipped him in the River Styx to make him invulnerable to attack. As an adult, he was killed by an arrow shot into his heel at the point his mother had held him, the one place the waters could not touch. From this story we get the term "Achilles' heel" to describe a weakness in an otherwise strong individual.

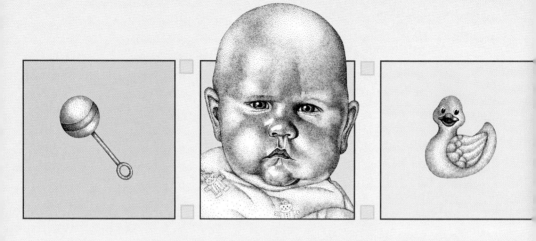

Who is the best-selling children's author in the world?

Dr. Suess, who has sold over 100,000,000 copies of his children's books. Dr. Suess's real name is Theodore Geisel, and he lived from 1904 to 1991. His books still sell in the millions.

At what age can you begin reading to a baby?

From birth—because it is never too early to read
to a baby. Just the sound of your voice is
comforting and infinitely pleasurable. And by the
time a baby is about six months old, it is likely to
show you how much it loves books, or at least how
much it loves chewing on them.

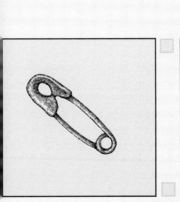
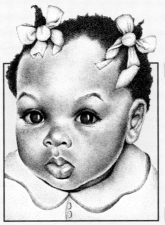
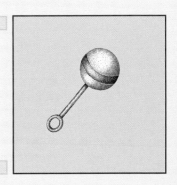

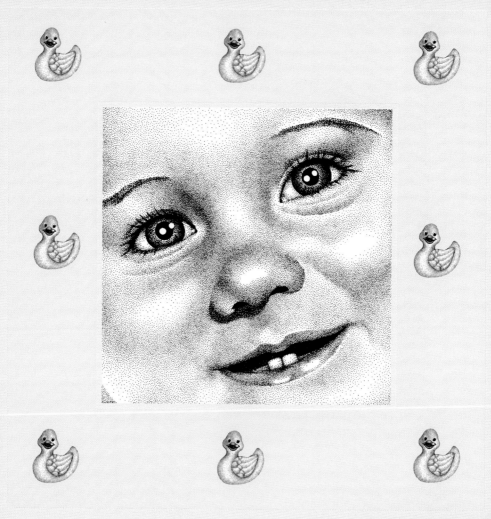

Who was the youngest baby to grow teeth?

In Denmark in 1970, a six-weeks-premature baby was born with eight teeth.

How many babies are born with teeth?

About one in every 2,000 babies is born with one or more teeth showing.

When do a baby's teeth normally appear?

Generally, (and even perfectly healthy babies may vary) the first teeth appear around five to eight months, first molars at 15 to 24 months.

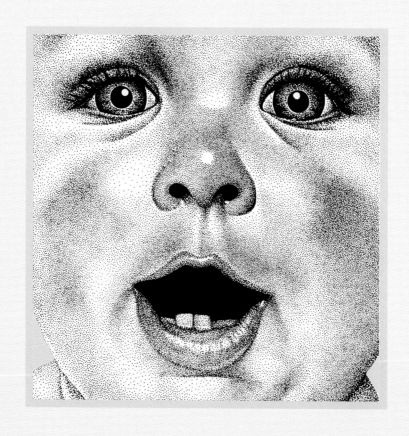

When a baby starts to grow teeth, which teeth typically appear first?

The two front bottom teeth grow in first for most babies.

At what age does a baby need a toothbrush?

Teething schedules are different for every baby, but a baby will probably have enough teeth to need a baby-sized toothbrush at 12 months.

At what age can the "average" baby put its foot in its mouth?

Around five months of age. This is a habit it is wise to discontinue in adult life, although it does demonstrate flexibility and considerable coordination.

At what age will a baby respond to being tickled?

Somewhere around three to five months.

How fast does a baby like to be rocked?

Researchers have spent a lot of time investigating the obvious and their discoveries are hardly surprising. The most soothing rhythm for infants seems to be around 70 gentle rocking movements per minute, very close to the 72 beats per minute of a mother's loving heart.

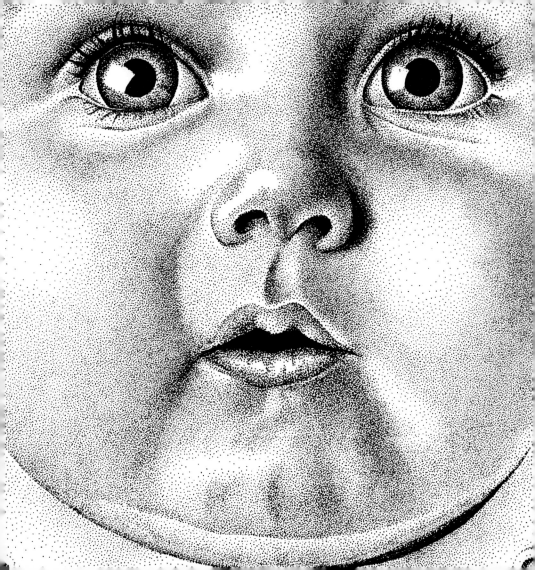

Where was the first baby hospital in the United States?

The first hospital designed exclusively for infants was founded in New York in 1887. It had eight beds.

What was the first commercially marketed baby powder in the United States?

Johnson's Baby Powder, introduced in 1893, was given away in the company's "Maternity Packets."

What is the most likely cause of a mother's neck, arm, and shoulder pain in the first few months following childbirth?

This commonly reported affliction is often due to the strain of carrying the baby, stroller, and diaper bag.

When a mother holds her baby, in which arm is she most likely to cradle it?

Mothers tend to cradle their babies in their left arms. This is true whether the mother is left-handed or right-handed. No one really knows why, but one theory is that mothers have a natural instinct to hold their babies close to their hearts.

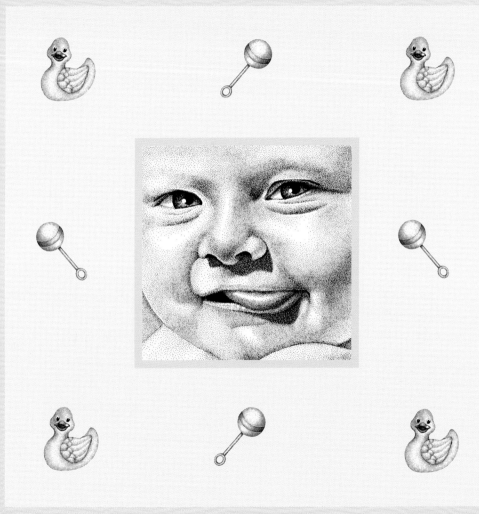

Can newborn babies smell?

Yes. In fact, the sense of smell in newborns is one their most developed senses.

Can a baby distinguish between its own mother's milk and someone else's?

Yes, it can smell the difference. Babies, naturally, prefer their own mother's milk.

Why don't young babies crave salty foods?

Because they can't taste them. The taste buds that detect salt don't develop until a baby is several months old.

How salty are a newborn baby's tears?

They aren't salty at all because although newborns cry, they don't make tears.

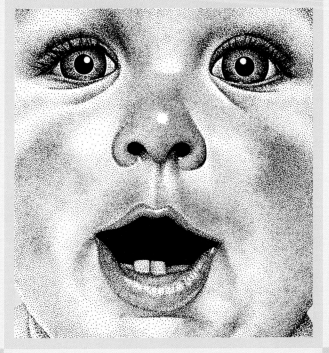

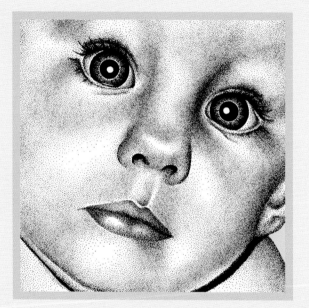

Where and when did the symbol of a baby representing the New Year originate?

A baby wearing a diaper and a banner representing the New Year dates to Germany in the 1300s. The symbol migrated to America with German immigrants.

What mythological baby made people fall in love by shooting arrows into their hearts?

Cupid.

What biblical baby was hidden by its mother in the bulrushes?

Moses.

Is a bowlegged baby a cause for alarm?

Almost never. Bowleggedness is perfectly normal for a little baby who has been curled up tightly inside its mother for nine months. After birth, the baby continues to "unfold," with legs and arms beginning to straighten out in about a week.

What does it mean if a newborn has bent ears?

Usually absolutely nothing. Most babies' ears are bent out of shape during the trip down the birth canal. Tiny ears usually regain their normal shape very quickly.

What is the best possible toy for a baby?

A caring, loving, playful adult.

Credits

The following sources provided photographs used as artist reference for the illustrations in this book:

Comstock; FPG: Michele-Salmieri; Indexstock Imagery; Liaison: Barbara Campbell, Franklin Avery; Stockbyte; Superstock, Inc; Weststock: Ken Anderson; Zephyr Images; Ani and Richard Couch; Mark Fox; Rick Helf; Denise Lawson; Joycelyn Calvin White.

The author wishes to thank Guinness World Records for permission to use several of the facts contained in this book.

The illustrations
in this book
were drawn by the author
using a
Rotring Rapidograph pen
on bristol paper.
The cover and book design are
by the author.

Original artwork
from this book
has been donated to
St. Jude Children's
Research
Hospital.

It will be sold to raise
money
for treatment and
research.